Cambridge **B2 First**

B2 Key Word Transformation

200 exam-styled practice exercises

Jane Turner

www.prosperityeducation.net

Registered offices: Sherlock Close, Cambridge
CB3 0HP, United Kingdom

© Prosperity Education Ltd. 2022

First published 2022

ISBN: 978-1-913825-71-3

This publication is in copyright. Subject to statutory exception and to the provisions of relevant collective licensing agreements, no reproduction of any part may take place without the written permission of Prosperity Education.

'Use of English', 'Cambridge B2 First' and 'FCE' are brands belonging to The Chancellor, Masters and Scholars of the University of Cambridge and are not associated with Prosperity Education or its products.

The moral rights of the author have been asserted.

For further information and resources, visit:
www.prosperityeducation.net

To infinity and beyond

Contents

Introduction	v
Test 1	1
Test 2	5
Test 3	9
Test 4	13
Test 5	17
Test 6	21
Test 7	25
Test 8	29
Test 9	33
Test 10	37
Test 11	41
Test 12	45
Test 13	49
Test 14	53
Test 15	57
Test 16	61
Test 17	65
Test 18	69
Test 19	73
Test 20	77
Answers	81

Introduction

Welcome to this edition of sample tests for the Cambridge B2 First, Part 4: Key Word Transformation, designed specifically for students preparing for the challenging Use of English section of the (FCE) examination, but also suitable for any English language student working at CEFR B2 level.

B2 results are given against the *Cambridge English Scale,* which is the average score for the four skills and the Use of English section of the test. In order to allow ample time for the reading parts (Parts 5–7) of Paper 1, it is advisable that candidates complete The Use of English section (Parts 1–4) as quickly as possible while maintaining accuracy.

This resource contains 200 exam-styled, single-sentence assessments, each carrying a lexical/lexico-grammatical focus, testing lexis, grammar and vocabulary. Each assessment comprises a sentence, followed by a 'key' word and an alternative sentence conveying the same meaning as the first but with a gap in the middle. Use the key word provided to complete the second sentence so that it has a similar meaning to the first sentence. You cannot change the keyword provided. Each correct answer is broken down into two marks. Next to each sentence transformation answer you will find a guide indicating the focus of the two parts of the answer: either G (grammatical) or L (lexical). This is a rough indication to help you with your revision for the exam.

Author **Jane Turner** is an associate lecturer in EAP/EFL at Anglia Ruskin University, Cambridge, and an EFL materials writer for international exam boards, universities and publishers. She previously worked as a Cambridge ESOL examiner for the British Council, and holds an MA in Educational Management and Cambridge CELTA and DELTA.

Visit www.prosperityeducation.net for more B2 First exam practice.

Cambridge B2 First
Use of English

Part 4

Test 1

Cambridge B2 First Use of English
Part 4 — Key word transformation — Test 1

For questions 1–10, complete the second sentence, using the word given, so that it has a similar meaning to the first sentence. Do not change the word provided and use between two and five words in total. In the separate answer sheet, write your answers in capital letters, using one box per letter.

1 Sarah lacks sufficient experience for this managerial role.

   ENOUGH

   Sarah is not _____ the manager.

2 Let's enjoy the sunny weather now because it's bound to turn colder soon.

   MOST

   We should make _____ the sunshine before it changes.

3 The school expects you to call the administrator if you're going to be absent.

   MEANT

   When you can't attend class, you _____ the school administrator.

4 It was definitely a mistake to have raised the issue of politics.

   BROUGHT

   If only I _____ politics as a subject.

5 I'm sure that we can persuade him to participate in the project.

INTO

He can _____ part in the project.

6 She apparently likes Jon because he respects women.

GETS

It would _____ with Jon due to his attitude towards women.

7 Completing the coursework is the only requirement for the course.

THAT

You will pass the course _____ all the assignments.

8 According to reports, the council is considering whether it should increase bus fares.

SAID

The council is _____ of a rise in bus fares.

9 I'm sure that the students were given an extra day to complete their projects.

HAVE

The teacher _____ the project deadline.

10 Pete's colleagues expect him to help them because he's too polite to refuse.

FOR

I think Pete _____ by his colleagues.

Answer sheet: Key word transformation Test No.

Name _____ Date _____

Write your answers in capital letters, using one box per letter.

1.

2.

3.

4.

5.

6.

7.

8.

9.

10.

Cambridge B2 First
Use of English

Part 4

Test 2

Cambridge B2 First Use of English
Part 4 — Key word transformation — **Test 2**

For questions 1–10, complete the second sentence, using the word given, so that it has a similar meaning to the first sentence. Do not change the word provided and use between two and five words in total. In the separate answer sheet, write your answers in capital letters, using one box per letter.

1 Before accepting the proposal, it's worth investigating the environmental implications.

   LOOKED

   Any potential impacts on nature _____ before the proposal is accepted.

2 I cannot see Maria accepting the company cutting her salary.

   PREPARED

   I don't think Maria is _____ in her salary.

3 She told the police that she wasn't a witness to the incident.

   CLAIMED

   When questioned by the police, she _____ the incident.

4 I just wanted to tell you how much I appreciate the help you've given me.

   SHOW

   I'd like to _____ all your help.

5 I warm up before matches to reduce the chance that I'll hurt myself.

GETTING

Warming up lessens my _____ injured during matches.

6 My bills are paid every month directly out of my bank account.

BASIS

I pay my bills _____ straight from my bank account.

7 You don't need to know what Sue and Carl were arguing about.

NOTHING

The reason for their argument has _____ you.

8 Alice certainly has the determination necessary to be a doctor.

THAT

Alice is _____ can definitely work as a doctor.

9 I don't want all of Mark's wild claims to fool you.

TAKEN

Please don't _____ by anything that Mark claims to have done

10 It's my twentieth anniversary as an employee here next week!

BEEN

Next week, I _____ for the company for twenty years.

Answer sheet: Key word transformation   Test No. ☐

Name _____   **Date** _____

Write your answers in capital letters, using one box per letter.

1. ☐☐☐☐☐☐☐☐☐☐☐☐☐☐☐
2. ☐☐☐☐☐☐☐☐☐☐☐☐☐☐☐
3. ☐☐☐☐☐☐☐☐☐☐☐☐☐☐☐
4. ☐☐☐☐☐☐☐☐☐☐☐☐☐☐☐
5. ☐☐☐☐☐☐☐☐☐☐☐☐☐☐☐
6. ☐☐☐☐☐☐☐☐☐☐☐☐☐☐☐
7. ☐☐☐☐☐☐☐☐☐☐☐☐☐☐☐
8. ☐☐☐☐☐☐☐☐☐☐☐☐☐☐☐
9. ☐☐☐☐☐☐☐☐☐☐☐☐☐☐☐
10. ☐☐☐☐☐☐☐☐☐☐☐☐☐☐☐

Cambridge B2 First
Use of English

Part 4

Test 3

Cambridge B2 First Use of English
Part 4 — Key word transformation — **Test 3**

For questions 1–10, complete the second sentence, using the word given, so that it has a similar meaning to the first sentence. Do not change the word provided and use between two and five words in total. In the separate answer sheet, write your answers in capital letters, using one box per letter.

1 When I saw you at the party, you behaved like we were complete strangers!

   NEVER

   You acted as _____ before at the party.

2 I would prefer not to give him my support until I have all the facts.

   BACK

   I'd rather not _____ knowing all the facts first.

3 Kate's teacher asked her to memorise the poem until she knew it word for word.

   HEART

   Kate had to _____ so that she could repeat it perfectly.

4 This section of the museum is just for French paintings.

   DEVOTED

   The museum _____ paintings by French artists.

5 I couldn't believe that you declined such a good offer.

SEE

It was a surprise to _____ down the offer.

6 Mum will be at the station to collect us, so I hope the train is on time.

WAITING

I hope the train isn't late as mum _____ us up.

7 The manager said that the team's poor sales were his fault.

BLAMED

The manager _____ his team's low sales.

8 I don't like being asked by my boss to do extra work for free.

WISH

I really _____ me to do unpaid overtime.

9 'Will I be able to ask questions at the end of the presentation?', asked Anna.

WHETHER

Anna wanted to know _____ the chance to ask questions after the presentation.

10 Though some people assume maths is boring, it can be very creative.

ACTUAL

Maths is assumed to be a boring subject, _____ it often requires creativity.

Answer sheet: Key word transformation　　　　Test No.

Name _____　　　Date _____

Write your answers in capital letters, using one box per letter.

1.
2.
3.
4.
5.
6.
7.
8.
9.
10.

Cambridge B2 First
Use of English

Part 4

Test 4

Cambridge B2 First Use of English
Part 4 — Key word transformation — Test 4

For questions 1–10, complete the second sentence, using the word given, so that it has a similar meaning to the first sentence. Do not change the word provided and use between two and five words in total. In the separate answer sheet, write your answers in capital letters, using one box per letter.

1 Unfortunately, Paul is not able to be creative when tackling problems.

   LACK

   Paul's _____ when solving problems is a pity.

2 Everyone knows that running is a great way to keep fit.

   KNOWN

   Running _____ effective form of exercise.

3 You cannot take part in the competition if you are under 18 years of age.

   QUALIFY

   In order _____, you need to be at least 18.

4 I'm not very strong and I'm quite slow, but I still enjoy doing sports.

   NOR

   Although I love doing sports, I _____ speed.

5 You called me exactly as I was getting ready to leave the house.

ABOUT

I _____ when you rang me.

6 Compared to all the other applicants, Maria was far better.

STOOD

Maria _____ else who applied for the job.

7 In the end, the police found out who was responsible for all the public disturbances.

BEEN

Officers eventually discovered _____ the disturbances in the neighbourhood.

8 My main task this week has been to finish my essay.

FOCUSING

This week I _____ completing my essay.

9 Sara shares her songs online hoping that producers will notice her talent.

HERSELF

By sharing her songs, Sara hopes _____ as a performer.

10 What he said about the company was a complete lie.

NO

There _____ his claims about the company.

Answer sheet: Key word transformation   Test No.

Name _____   **Date** _____

Write your answers in capital letters, using one box per letter.

1.
2.
3.
4.
5.
6.
7.
8.
9.
10.

Cambridge B2 First

Use of English

Part 4

Test 5

Cambridge B2 First Use of English
Part 4 — Key word transformation — **Test 5**

For questions 1–10, complete the second sentence, using the word given, so that it has a similar meaning to the first sentence. Do not change the word provided and use between two and five words in total. In the separate answer sheet, write your answers in capital letters, using one box per letter.

1 State the name of the institution you are representing on the form.

   WHICH

   Please indicate on the form _____ belong.

2 Jess is both a theatre director and a singer.

   DOES

   In her career, not _____ plays, but she also sings.

3 All the wet weather lately has helped local farmers.

   BENEFITTED

   In the local area, _____ the recent wet weather.

4 It was wrong of you to permit the students to leave their class early.

   GIVEN

   The students should _____ to leave early.

5 My concerns about how we are destroying the planet are growing day by day.

INCREASINGLY

I am _____ of the planet.

6 If you want to play music here, that's fine by me.

MIND

I don't _____ music here if that's what you want to do.

7 I checked my watch and realised it was much later than I'd expected.

TRACK

I realised I had completely _____ when I looked at my watch.

8 It was the most embarrassing moment in my life.

SUCH

Never _____ before.

9 You don't have any evidence but I still believe you.

WORD

I'm willing _____ it despite the lack of proof.

10 As far as I know, Peter's not working today.

KNOWLEDGE

To the _____, today is Peter's day off.

Answer sheet: Key word transformation　　　　Test No.

Name _____　　**Date** _____

Write your answers in capital letters, using one box per letter.

1.
2.
3.
4.
5.
6.
7.
8.
9.
10.

Cambridge B2 First
Use of English

Part 4

Test 6

Cambridge B2 First Use of English
Part 4 — Key word transformation — **Test 6**

For questions 1–10, complete the second sentence, using the word given, so that it has a similar meaning to the first sentence. Do not change the word provided and use between two and five words in total. In the separate answer sheet, write your answers in capital letters, using one box per letter.

1. You could barely see the stain after we had cleaned the carpet.

   VIRTUALLY

   The stain _____ after cleaning the carpet.

2. I've just found out about Tom and Ruth deciding not to get married.

   CALL

   I've just heard that Tom and Ruth _____ their wedding.

3. I worked on that project for ages but nobody thanked me.

   THANKS

   I _____ all the work I did on that project.

4. I'm relieved that you didn't have an injury, but next time be more careful.

   YOURSELF

   You _____, so next time don't be so careless.

5 After a terrible start to the year, we're now selling double the number of products.

SINCE

Our _____ the beginning of the year.

6 I thought Max had a lot of money until I met him.

UNDER

Before meeting Max, I had _____ that he was wealthy.

7 It's absolutely vital that we win this match.

COSTS

We need _____ because it's such an important match.

8 The sound problems didn't affect how much the audience enjoyed the show.

DIFFERENCE

I don't think the sound problems _____ the audience's enjoyment of the show.

9 You must not mention the party to Ed because it will spoil the surprise.

CIRCUMSTANCES

Remember that under _____ Ed about the party.

10 Unfortunately, it's impossible to put off writing the report any longer.

AVOID

I'm afraid you _____ the report now.

Answer sheet: Key word transformation Test No.

Name _____   **Date** _____

Write your answers in capital letters, using one box per letter.

1.

2.

3.

4.

5.

6.

7.

8.

9.

10.

Cambridge B2 First
Use of English

Part 4

Test 7

Cambridge B2 First Use of English
Part 4 — Key word transformation — Test 7

For questions 1–10, complete the second sentence, using the word given, so that it has a similar meaning to the first sentence. Do not change the word provided and use between two and five words in total. In the separate answer sheet, write your answers in capital letters, using one box per letter.

1. We really appreciate how much you contributed during the project.

    MADE

    We are very grateful for the _____ to the project.

2. I didn't think of borrowing the money from the bank.

    CROSSED

    It never _____ a bank loan.

3. Given the condition of the house, the previous owner clearly spent a lot of money on it.

    MUST

    Lots of money _____ on this house.

4. We tend to feel angry when our parents don't listen to us.

    CAN

    We _____ towards our parents for ignoring us.

5 You'll arrive far sooner if you avoid the city centre.

MUCH

Your journey _____ you don't go.

6 I travelled far more in the past.

AS

Nowadays, I don't travel _____ to.

7 You cannot follow the course because you don't have access to the internet.

MAKES

Having no access to the internet _____ to follow the course.

8 Children should have role models they can admire, like parents or teachers.

LOOK

Children need someone to _____ as their parents or teachers.

9 I need to complete the report by tomorrow.

GET

I have _____ by the deadline.

10 Many people are confused about the proposed car-sharing scheme.

DEAL

There is a _____ concerning the new scheme.

Answer sheet: Key word transformation Test No. ☐

Name _____ **Date** _____

Write your answers in capital letters, using one box per letter.

1. ☐☐☐☐☐☐☐☐☐☐☐☐☐☐
   ☐☐☐☐☐☐☐☐☐☐☐☐☐☐

2. ☐☐☐☐☐☐☐☐☐☐☐☐☐☐
   ☐☐☐☐☐☐☐☐☐☐☐☐☐☐

3. ☐☐☐☐☐☐☐☐☐☐☐☐☐☐
   ☐☐☐☐☐☐☐☐☐☐☐☐☐☐

4. ☐☐☐☐☐☐☐☐☐☐☐☐☐☐
   ☐☐☐☐☐☐☐☐☐☐☐☐☐☐

5. ☐☐☐☐☐☐☐☐☐☐☐☐☐☐
   ☐☐☐☐☐☐☐☐☐☐☐☐☐☐

6. ☐☐☐☐☐☐☐☐☐☐☐☐☐☐
   ☐☐☐☐☐☐☐☐☐☐☐☐☐☐

7. ☐☐☐☐☐☐☐☐☐☐☐☐☐☐
   ☐☐☐☐☐☐☐☐☐☐☐☐☐☐

8. ☐☐☐☐☐☐☐☐☐☐☐☐☐☐
   ☐☐☐☐☐☐☐☐☐☐☐☐☐☐

9. ☐☐☐☐☐☐☐☐☐☐☐☐☐☐
   ☐☐☐☐☐☐☐☐☐☐☐☐☐☐

10. ☐☐☐☐☐☐☐☐☐☐☐☐☐☐
    ☐☐☐☐☐☐☐☐☐☐☐☐☐☐

Cambridge B2 First
Use of English

Part 4

Test 8

Cambridge B2 First Use of English
Part 4 — Key word transformation — Test 8

For questions 1–10, complete the second sentence, using the word given, so that it has a similar meaning to the first sentence. Do not change the word provided and use between two and five words in total. In the separate answer sheet, write your answers in capital letters, using one box per letter.

1 When I was young, most children invented games rather than buying expensive toys.

   WOULD

   In the past, _____ with their own games to play.

2 For our research, we are looking for learners of the English language.

   NATIVE

   We would like to interview people _____ not English.

3 You can't deny that there has never been anyone else as good as him at our club.

   REGARDED

   In our club's history, he must surely _____ player.

4 You're always borrowing money from me, and I've had enough.

   SICK

   I'm getting _____ me for money.

5 You really can't justify not going to the meeting.

   EXCUSE

   There is _____ the meeting.

6 Julie has invested her money wisely for her retirement.

   WISE

   Julie _____ for when she retires.

7 The president will apologise formally to the prime minister shortly.

   RECEIVE

   The prime minister is set _____ soon.

8 I don't like it when my neighbours wake me up by playing loud music.

   OBJECT

   I really _____ by my neighbours' loud music.

9 Ben might need to explain to us why he has been behaving so strangely.

   OWE

   Ben may _____ his odd behaviour.

10 According to the media, the museum lost several rare vases in the burglary.

   REPORTED

   Thieves _____ rare vases from the museum.

Answer sheet: Key word transformation Test No. ☐

Name _____ **Date** _____

Write your answers in capital letters, using one box per letter.

1. ☐☐☐☐☐☐☐☐☐☐☐☐☐☐☐
2. ☐☐☐☐☐☐☐☐☐☐☐☐☐☐☐
3. ☐☐☐☐☐☐☐☐☐☐☐☐☐☐☐
4. ☐☐☐☐☐☐☐☐☐☐☐☐☐☐☐
5. ☐☐☐☐☐☐☐☐☐☐☐☐☐☐☐
6. ☐☐☐☐☐☐☐☐☐☐☐☐☐☐☐
7. ☐☐☐☐☐☐☐☐☐☐☐☐☐☐☐
8. ☐☐☐☐☐☐☐☐☐☐☐☐☐☐☐
9. ☐☐☐☐☐☐☐☐☐☐☐☐☐☐☐
10. ☐☐☐☐☐☐☐☐☐☐☐☐☐☐☐

Cambridge B2 First

Use of English

Part 4

Test 9

Cambridge B2 First Use of English
Part 4 — Key word transformation — Test 9

For questions 1–10, complete the second sentence, using the word given, so that it has a similar meaning to the first sentence. Do not change the word provided and use between two and five words in total. In the separate answer sheet, write your answers in capital letters, using one box per letter.

1 Managers should make sure that all the work is divided fairly.

   LABOUR

   Ensuring that there is a _____ is the manager's job.

2 Many people demonstrated because they disagreed with the company constructing a new factory.

   DEMONSTRATIONS

   There were many _____ of the factory.

3 Many of my paintings have been inspired by African art.

   SOURCE

   African art has _____ to me as a painter.

4 I like the fact that everyone who works here looks after their colleagues.

   ONE

   It is pleasing to see people _____ at work.

5 If I had failed that exam, I might have needed to change my university subject.

MEANT

Failing that exam _____ my choice of degree course.

6 I don't think they will be willing to compromise.

IMAGINE

I just _____ a compromise.

7 Unfortunately, I found the film to be quite disappointing.

LIVED

I wish the film _____ to my expectations.

8 I tend to like rock music more than jazz music.

OVER

I usually have _____ jazz.

9 When my boss fired me, I realised that it was time for a career change.

SACK

After being _____ I decided to change my career.

10 I'm pretty sure that Lisa is dealing with a complaint from a customer.

SEEING

Lisa must _____ an unhappy customer.

Answer sheet: Key word transformation Test No.

Name _____ Date _____

Write your answers in capital letters, using one box per letter.

1.
2.
3.
4.
5.
6.
7.
8.
9.
10.

Cambridge B2 First
Use of English

Part 4

Test 10

Cambridge B2 First Use of English
Part 4 — Key word transformation — Test 10

For questions 1–10, complete the second sentence, using the word given, so that it has a similar meaning to the first sentence. Do not change the word provided and use between two and five words in total. In the separate answer sheet, write your answers in capital letters, using one box per letter.

1 I will never forget Mr Piper's science lessons because they were so enjoyable.

   FUN

   I will always _____ during Mr Piper's classes.

2 If you like, you can bring your sister along too.

   MIND

   I _____ us on the trip.

3 Officials are investigating what had caused the accident.

   INVESTIGATION

   A formal _____ to discover the causes of the accident.

4 Some people cannot see blue and green as different colours.

   DISTINGUISH

   Some people are _____ blue and green.

5 You absolutely must not bring phones into the exam room.

STRICTLY

It _____ phones into the exam venue.

6 I get most of my protein from fish rather than from meat.

CHIEF

Meat is not _____ protein, fish is.

7 I'd always go for a job with a decent salary above anything else.

COUNTS

I think the rate _____ the most when choosing a job.

8 I think, by that point, we'll be into the fifth hour of the flight.

BEEN

By that time, we _____ for several hours.

9 The detective was always impatient with people who wasted the police's time.

LITTLE

The detective had _____ anyone he viewed as a timewaster.

10 You will have access to all kinds of resources while you're doing the project.

DISPOSAL

A range of resources will _____ during the project.

Answer sheet: Key word transformation Test No.

Name _____   **Date** _____

Write your answers in capital letters, using one box per letter.

1
2
3
4
5
6
7
8
9
10

Cambridge B2 First

Use of English

Part 4

Test 11

Cambridge B2 First Use of English
Part 4 — Key word transformation — **Test 11**

For questions 1–10, complete the second sentence, using the word given, so that it has a similar meaning to the first sentence. Do not change the word provided and use between two and five words in total. In the separate answer sheet, write your answers in capital letters, using one box per letter.

1 When Tom was awarded the top prize, it was very important to him.

   AWARD

   Being _____ everything to Tom.

2 We have different views on politics, but that shouldn't damage our friendship.

   FALL

   Let's _____ the subject of politics – we can agree to disagree.

3 Money obviously does not automatically lead to happiness.

   SEEMS

   It _____ no guarantee of happiness.

4 A statement from the prime minister's office is expected shortly.

   BE

   The prime minister's office should _____ any moment now.

5 Not preparing in advance led to several problems during the presentation.

   BEEN

   The problems we experienced _____ with a bit of preparation.

6 After much consideration, university seems to be the best option for me.

   OPTIONS

   Having _____, I've chosen to go to university.

7 I didn't go to the party after developing a nasty case of flu.

   COME

   I missed the party because I _____ flu.

8 The manager's visit was the wrong time for a discussion about salaries.

   BRING

   We decided not _____ the manager was visiting.

9 The sooner you apply, the better in my opinion.

   ADVISE

   I would _____ your application to the administrator as soon as possible.

10 We will add up the scores you achieved in each course component.

   COMBINATION

   Your final grade will _____ your scores for various elements of the course.

Answer sheet: Key word transformation Test No.

Name _____ **Date** _____

Write your answers in capital letters, using one box per letter.

1.
2.
3.
4.
5.
6.
7.
8.
9.
10.

Cambridge B2 First
Use of English

Part 4

Test 12

Cambridge B2 First Use of English
Part 4 — Key word transformation — **Test 12**

For questions 1–10, complete the second sentence, using the word given, so that it has a similar meaning to the first sentence. Do not change the word provided and use between two and five words in total. In the separate answer sheet, write your answers in capital letters, using one box per letter.

1. I'll take the bus tomorrow while the mechanic fixes the tyre on my car.

   HAVING

   Tomorrow I'm _____ so I'll come to work by bus.

2. If we don't act immediately, it is unlikely that there will be any growth in our sales.

   UNLESS

   Our sales won't _____ action to improve things.

3. I was anxious about getting to the airport late, so I set several alarms.

   AS

   I set more than one alarm so _____ my flight.

4. The proposal seems logical from a financial perspective.

   SENSE

   In terms of costs, the idea _____ me.

5 I don't have the energy for the gym tonight, so I'll go tomorrow instead.

BOTHERED

I simply _____ out tonight.

6 The welcome party enabled the students to get to know each other.

ICE

The students were able _____ at the welcome party.

7 Claire only went vegetarian to support her husband's new lifestyle.

MEAT

Claire _____ her husband hadn't changed his diet.

8 Even though I put in so much effort, physics is still impossible to me.

MATTER

I can never understand physics, _____ try.

9 The building costs should be calculated first.

WORKED

Construction costs _____ before anything else.

10 We couldn't manage to climb the mountain because of the weather conditions.

FAILURE

Our attempt to reach the top ended _____ to the weather.

Answer sheet: Key word transformation Test No. [ ]

Name _____ **Date** _____

Write your answers in capital letters, using one box per letter.

1.
2.
3.
4.
5.
6.
7.
8.
9.
10.

Cambridge B2 First
Use of English

Part 4

Test 13

Cambridge B2 First Use of English

Part 4 — Key word transformation — **Test 13**

For questions 1–10, complete the second sentence, using the word given, so that it has a similar meaning to the first sentence. Do not change the word provided and use between two and five words in total. In the separate answer sheet, write your answers in capital letters, using one box per letter.

1 Coming to work when you were clearly unwell was the wrong decision.

   SICK

   You should _____ today because you were unwell.

2 Ali spent the whole evening teasing me about my accent, which was strange.

   FUN

   I didn't understand why Ali _____ I spoke.

3 The conference will be in the city centre so that it's easier for everyone to reach.

   SAKE

   For the _____, we've chosen a central location.

4 Even though a lot of people criticised the project, it turned out well.

   SPITE

   Overall, in _____, the project was successful.

5 The laptop wasn't available anywhere, so I couldn't buy it.

STOCK

If only the laptop _____, I would have bought it.

6 Sadly, the college has not accepted me onto the course I applied for.

DECLINED

My _____, which is a pity.

7 It was impossible to hear the discussion from the back of the lecture room.

CATCH

I could _____ discussed during the lecture.

8 Your essay would be better if it was more detailed.

DEPTH

If I were you, I would _____ in your essay.

9 I do not regret studying philosophy at university at all.

ABSOLUTELY

I have _____ my choice of degree.

10 We will need to be quite direct if we want Jim's help.

STRAIGHT

Let's _____ point when asking Jim for a favour.

Answer sheet: Key word transformation Test No.

Name _____ Date _____

Write your answers in capital letters, using one box per letter.

1
2
3
4
5
6
7
8
9
10

Cambridge B2 First
Use of English

Part 4

Test 14

Cambridge B2 First Use of English
Part 4   Key word transformation   **Test 14**

For questions 1–10, complete the second sentence, using the word given, so that it has a similar meaning to the first sentence. Do not change the word provided and use between two and five words in total. In the separate answer sheet, write your answers in capital letters, using one box per letter.

1   The sound of the children's laughter coming from the garden was a relief.

LAUGHING

I was happy that I could _____ in the garden.

2   It's annoying when you ignore me while I'm telling you something.

APPRECIATE

I do not _____ while I'm talking to you.

3   I think Zoe's course is far easier compared to the one that Tony is doing.

CHALLENGE

Tony's course seems to offer much _____ than Zoe's.

4   'I have met so many famous people,' said Anna.

BOASTED

Anna _____ several celebrities.

5 You arrived at 10am, which was far too late.

TURNED

You should _____ much earlier than you did.

6 'Richard didn't get the news from me,' said Louise.

TELLING

Louise _____ about the news.

7 I was less eager to apply when I saw what the role actually involved.

PUT

The job responsibilities _____ applying for the role.

8 I know that you will find the time for it at some point.

ROUND

I'm sure that you will _____ eventually.

9 I made some changes to the recipe because I wanted the children to like it.

SUIT

The recipe was _____ the children's tastes.

10 Seeing Sara giving her first theatre performance is something I'll never forget.

SIGHT

I'll always remember _____ on stage for the first time.

Answer sheet: Key word transformation　　　　Test No. ☐

Name _____　　**Date** _____

Write your answers in capital letters, using one box per letter.

1.
2.
3.
4.
5.
6.
7.
8.
9.
10.

Cambridge B2 First
Use of English

Part 4

Test 15

Cambridge B2 First Use of English
Part 4   Key word transformation   **Test 15**

For questions 1–10, complete the second sentence, using the word given, so that it has a similar meaning to the first sentence. Do not change the word provided and use between two and five words in total. In the separate answer sheet, write your answers in capital letters, using one box per letter.

1. I've never met anyone who dresses like Laura.

   TASTE

   Laura's _____ clothes is unique.

2. I was so relieved when I finally passed my driving test.

   SUCH

   It _____ get my driving licence.

3. Generally, information taken from blogs is not suitable for university essays.

   SOURCE

   Blogs are an _____ for academic essays.

4. Apparently, my grandfather did not like his government job.

   SAID

   My grandfather was _____ for the government.

5 While I'm away, Monica is going to look after the team.

   EYE

   Monica will be _____ the team in my absence.

6 The most important thing in this job is being confident.

   MATTERS

   Having confidence is _____ most in this type of work.

7 Most athletes have retired by the time they are forty.

   FEW

   There are _____ into their forties.

8 It is easier to get a job if you have a university degree.

   LIKELY

   University graduates _____ employment.

9 Ed's presentation will start shortly.

   ABOUT

   Ed _____ a presentation to his colleagues.

10 We wanted you to keep the meeting secret.

   SUPPOSED

   You were _____ anyone about the meeting.

Answer sheet: Key word transformation   **Test No.** ☐

Name _____   **Date** _____

Write your answers in capital letters, using one box per letter.

1.
2.
3.
4.
5.
6.
7.
8.
9.
10.

Cambridge B2 First

Use of English

Part 4

Test 16

Cambridge B2 First Use of English
Part 4 — Key word transformation — **Test 16**

For questions 1–10, complete the second sentence, using the word given, so that it has a similar meaning to the first sentence. Do not change the word provided and use between two and five words in total. In the separate answer sheet, write your answers in capital letters, using one box per letter.

1 If you learn a language, it will eventually improve your career opportunities.

   RUN

   Learning a language will help you _____ with your career.

2 I wish I had learnt to play the piano when I had the chance as a child.

   REGRET

   I _____ piano lessons in my youth.

3 'You were one who ate the last slice of pizza,' Isabel said to Oana.

   ACCUSED

   Isabel _____ the pizza.

4 Julia will receive her nursing qualification in December.

   HAVE

   Julia _____ as a nurse by the end of the year.

5 I enjoy thinking about the holidays I spent with my grandparents.

FOND

I have many _____ holidays with my grandparents.

6 I definitely think it would be worth drinking less coffee every day.

CUT

You really ought _____ on the amount of coffee you drink.

7 The government has not decided what to do yet.

BEEN

The final decision _____ by the government yet.

8 Gym membership gives you access to all the fitness classes at no extra cost.

ENTITLED

Gym members _____ any exercise class for free.

9 Going to Japan last year was my first ever time on a plane.

NEVER

I _____ last year's trip to Japan.

10 We couldn't hear our TV properly because of the music in the apartment next door.

MADE

Our neighbours' music _____ us to watch TV.

Answer sheet: Key word transformation　　　　Test No.

Name _____　　**Date** _____

Write your answers in capital letters, using one box per letter.

1.
2.
3.
4.
5.
6.
7.
8.
9.
10.

Cambridge B2 First
Use of English

Part 4

Test 17

Cambridge B2 First Use of English
Part 4 — Key word transformation — **Test 17**

For questions 1–10, complete the second sentence, using the word given, so that it has a similar meaning to the first sentence. Do not change the word provided and use between two and five words in total. In the separate answer sheet, write your answers in capital letters, using one box per letter.

1. I was so excited that I bought too much.

   CARRIED

   I _____ when I was in the shop.

2. One of the worst parts of my job is when I have to write sales reports.

   STAND

   I _____ sales reports at work.

3. I think there needs to be a different approach to solving this problem.

   MUST

   A new approach _____ if we want to solve the problem.

4. This car park is strictly reserved for members of staff.

   RIGHT

   Only employees _____ their cars here.

5 July is the most popular time for guests to book rooms at our hotel.

TEND

We _____ more guests in our hotel in July.

6 Internet advertising really helped my business to be successful.

TOOK

My business _____ after I started to advertise it online.

7 'I have a lesson this morning so please don't call me,' Marcus said to Isla.

TOLD

Marcus _____ him while he was having his lesson.

8 Anton is busy with his job search at the moment.

TRYING

Currently, Anton _____ a new job.

9 Hearing about Max's travels in America made me interested to visit the country.

TEMPTED

After talking to Max _____ a holiday in the USA.

10 Honesty simply does not exist in modern politics.

SUCH

There is _____ a politician who is honest with people.

Answer sheet: Key word transformation Test No.

Name _____ **Date** _____

Write your answers in capital letters, using one box per letter.

1.
2.
3.
4.
5.
6.
7.
8.
9.
10.

Cambridge B2 First

Use of English

Part 4

Test 18

Cambridge B2 First Use of English
Part 4 Key word transformation **Test 18**

For questions 1–10, complete the second sentence, using the word given, so that it has a similar meaning to the first sentence. Do not change the word provided and use between two and five words in total. In the separate answer sheet, write your answers in capital letters, using one box per letter.

1 We are getting ready for the publication of Dr Wilson's new book next month.

   BE

   Dr Wilson's next book _____ next month.

2 It should be remembered that students have different learning styles.

   MIND

   It is worth _____ we all learn in different ways.

3 I'm impressed by Jack's recent suggestions in our team meetings.

   COME

   In our recent meetings, Jack _____ some excellent ideas.

4 My legs are far stronger than my upper body.

   SAME

   My upper body does not have the _____ my legs.

5 The volunteer project has made it more likely that the birds will survive.

CHANCE

The birds now have a _____ thanks to the project.

6 She did not intend to alter her diet in any way.

INTENTION

She had absolutely _____ her diet.

7 We received all the necessary information from Tina.

WITH

Tina _____ we needed.

8 Action is required if we want to protect this species.

DIE

This species _____ completely unless action is taken.

9 The only reason I recognised Lisa was because of her red coat.

WEARING

If Lisa _____ her red coat, I would not have recognised her.

10 The band's combination of rock and jazz styles has been very successful.

SUCCESSFULLY

The band _____ jazz in their music.

Answer sheet: Key word transformation　　　　Test No. ☐

Name _____　　**Date** _____

Write your answers in capital letters, using one box per letter.

1.
2.
3.
4.
5.
6.
7.
8.
9.
10.

Cambridge B2 First

Use of English

Part 4

Test 19

Cambridge B2 First Use of English
Part 4 — Key word transformation — Test 19

For questions 1–10, complete the second sentence, using the word given, so that it has a similar meaning to the first sentence. Do not change the word provided and use between two and five words in total. In the separate answer sheet, write your answers in capital letters, using one box per letter.

1 John does not seem to be determined enough to have a professional sports career.

   LACK

   John seems to _____ a professional athlete.

2 The club changed its name from Wickmore United to Wickmore Athletic.

   FORMERLY

   The club _____ as Wickmore United.

3 Exercise will be a compulsory part of this programme.

   FORCED

   Programme participants _____ regular exercise.

4 I like Kaspar's willingness to give new things a try.

   ALWAYS

   Kaspar _____ new things, which is great.

5 It's not fair when parents expect so much of their children.

PUT

I think that parents should _____ on their children.

6 I was breathing pretty quickly after climbing all those stairs.

BREATH

I _____ after I had gone up all those stairs.

7 Television may affect children in a positive way.

INFLUENCE

Some TV shows can have _____ children.

8 They don't sell the video games together with the console.

SEPARATELY

The video games _____ the console.

9 I only wanted to learn Italian after meeting Mario.

THOUGHT

I _____ learning Italian until I met Mario.

10 It is possible that Tom invented everything simply to make people laugh.

MADE

Tom _____ just as a joke.

Answer sheet: Key word transformation Test No.

Name _____ **Date** _____

Write your answers in capital letters, using one box per letter.

1.
2.
3.
4.
5.
6.
7.
8.
9.
10.

Cambridge B2 First
Use of English

Part 4

Test 20

Cambridge B2 First Use of English

Part 4 — Key word transformation — **Test 20**

For questions 1–10, complete the second sentence, using the word given, so that it has a similar meaning to the first sentence. Do not change the word provided and use between two and five words in total. In the separate answer sheet, write your answers in capital letters, using one box per letter.

1 After much debate, the ministers agreed on the best solution to the problem.

   AGREEMENT

   The ministers were eventually _____ should be done.

2 I would be happy to answer any questions you may have.

   CONTACT

   Please do not _____ you have any questions.

3 No other cheap shoes look as smart as these ones.

   THAT

   This is the _____ get for such a cheap price.

4 I found that yoga benefitted me a lot when I tried it.

   PROVED

   I decided to try yoga, _____ be very beneficial.

5 If you tell us where you live, we can collect you from your home.

PROVIDING

We can pick you up _____ directions to your house.

6 Only fifty places were available for the trip.

LIMITED

The number of places on the trip _____ fifty.

7 While I missed the penalty, I did score three goals.

MADE

Scoring three goals _____ missing the penalty.

8 Buses are by far the most convenient way to get around cities.

MOST

Taking the bus offers _____ travelling in cities.

9 It pleased her to hit the ball with all her power.

PLEASURE

She _____ the ball as hard as she could.

10 Our lack of practice was the only reason we didn't win.

HAVE

We _____ them easily if we had practised more.

Answer sheet: Key word transformation   Test No. ☐

Name _____   **Date** _____

Write your answers in capital letters, using one box per letter.

1. ☐☐☐☐☐☐☐☐☐☐☐☐☐☐☐
   ☐☐☐☐☐☐☐☐☐☐☐☐☐☐☐

2. ☐☐☐☐☐☐☐☐☐☐☐☐☐☐☐
   ☐☐☐☐☐☐☐☐☐☐☐☐☐☐☐

3. ☐☐☐☐☐☐☐☐☐☐☐☐☐☐☐
   ☐☐☐☐☐☐☐☐☐☐☐☐☐☐☐

4. ☐☐☐☐☐☐☐☐☐☐☐☐☐☐☐
   ☐☐☐☐☐☐☐☐☐☐☐☐☐☐☐

5. ☐☐☐☐☐☐☐☐☐☐☐☐☐☐☐
   ☐☐☐☐☐☐☐☐☐☐☐☐☐☐☐

6. ☐☐☐☐☐☐☐☐☐☐☐☐☐☐☐
   ☐☐☐☐☐☐☐☐☐☐☐☐☐☐☐

7. ☐☐☐☐☐☐☐☐☐☐☐☐☐☐☐
   ☐☐☐☐☐☐☐☐☐☐☐☐☐☐☐

8. ☐☐☐☐☐☐☐☐☐☐☐☐☐☐☐
   ☐☐☐☐☐☐☐☐☐☐☐☐☐☐☐

9. ☐☐☐☐☐☐☐☐☐☐☐☐☐☐☐
   ☐☐☐☐☐☐☐☐☐☐☐☐☐☐☐

10. ☐☐☐☐☐☐☐☐☐☐☐☐☐☐☐
    ☐☐☐☐☐☐☐☐☐☐☐☐☐☐☐

Answers

Answers — Key word transformation — Test 1

1	experienced enough	to be	L	G
2	the most	(out) of	L	G
3	are meant	to call	L	G
4	had not / hadn't	brought up	G	L
5	be talked into	taking	G	L
6	appear/seem (that)	she gets on	G	L
7	provided/assuming that	you complete	L	G
8	said to be	thinking	G	L
9	must have	extended	G	L
10	is / is being	taken for granted	G	L

Answers — Key word transformation — Test 2

1	should be	looked into/at	G	L
2	prepared to accept	a cut/decrease/reduction	G	L
3	claimed she had not / claimed not to have	witnessed	G	L
4	show (my) appreciation	for	L	G
5	risk/chance/chances	of getting	L	G
6	on a	monthly basis	G	L
7	(got) nothing	to do with	L	G
8	(so) determined	that she	L	G
9	be	taken in	G	L
10	will have been	working	G	L

Answers — Key word transformation — Test 3

1	if/though	we had never met	L	G
2	back him (up)	without	L	G
3	learn/memorise the poem	by heart	L	G
4	has devoted	this section to	G	L
5	see you	had turned / turning / turn	G	L
6	will be waiting	to pick	G	L
7	blamed	himself for	L	G
8	wish my boss	wouldn't/didn't ask	L	G
9	whether	she would have/get/be given / there would be	G	L
10	but	in actual fact	G	L

Answers — Key word transformation — Test 4

1	lack of	creativity / creative ability	G	L
2	is	well known as an / known to be an / known as an	L	G
3	to qualify for	the/this competition	G	L
4	have	neither strength nor	G	L
5	was (just) about	to leave	L	G
6	stood out	from everyone	L	G
7	who had been	causing / responsible for	G	L
8	have (mainly) been	focusing on	L	G
9	to get herself	noticed	G	L
10	was no	truth in	G	L

Answers — Key word transformation — Test 5

#				
1	the institution	to which you	G	L
2	only does Jess/she	direct	G	L
3	farmers have	benefitted from	G	L
4	not have been	given permission	G	L
5	increasingly concerned about	the destruction	G	L
6	mind	you playing / if you play	L	G
7	lost	track of (the) time	G	L
8	had I felt/experienced	such embarrassment	G	L
9	to take	your word for	G	L
10	best of	my knowledge	G	L

Answers — Key word transformation — Test 6

#				
1	was/became	virtually invisible	G	L
2	have decided to	call off	G	L
3	received/got/had	no thanks for	L	G
4	could have	injured / hurt yourself	G	L
5	sales	have doubled since	L	G
6	been	under the impression	G	L
7	to win	at all costs	G	L
8	made	any difference to / a difference to	L	G
9	no circumstances	should you tell	L	G
10	can't/cannot avoid	writing	L	G

Answers — Key word transformation — Test 7

#				
1	contribution	you (have) made / that you (have) made	L	G
2	crossed my mind	to get/take out	L	G
3	must have been	spent	G	L
4	can (often) feel	anger	G	L
5	will be	much quicker/faster if / much quicker/faster providing	G	L
6	as much/often as	I used	G	L
7	makes it	impossible (for you)	G	L
8	look up to	such	G	L
9	to get	the report finished/completed	G	L
10	great/good deal of	confusion	G	L

Answers — Key word transformation — Test 8

#				
1	children would	come up	G	L
2	whose	native language/tongue is	G	L
3	be regarded as	the greatest/best	L	G
4	sick of	you (always) asking	G	L
5	no excuse for	(you) missing / not attending	L	G
6	has made (some)	wise investments	G	L
7	to receive	a formal apology	G	L
8	object to	being woken up	L	G
9	owe us	an explanation for	G	L
10	are reported	to have stolen/taken	L	G

Answers — Key word transformation — Test 9

#				
1	fair	division of labour	G	L
2	demonstrations (held) against/about	the construction	G	L
3	been	the/a source of inspiration	G	L
4	looking after	one another	G	L
5	might/could/may have	meant changing	G	L
6	can't/cannot imagine them	reaching/making	G	L
7	had	lived up	G	L
8	a preference for	rock over	L	G
9	given	the sack	G	L
10	be	seeing to	G	L

Answers — Key word transformation — Test 10

#				
1	remember having	fun / so much fun / the fun I had	G	L
2	don't/do not mind / wouldn't/would not mind	your sister joining / if your sister joined	L	G
3	investigation is	being held/carried out/conducted / taking place / underway	G	L
4	unable to	distinguish between	G	L
5	is strictly forbidden / is strictly prohibited	to bring	L	G
6	my chief	source of	G	L
7	of pay	is what counts / counts	L	G
8	will have been	flying	G	L
9	little patience	for	L	G
10	be	at your disposal	G	L

Answers — Key word transformation — Test 11

1	given the (top) award	meant	G	L
2	not fall	out over	G	L
3	seems (obvious) that	money is/brings/offers/provides	L	G
4	be issuing/making/releasing	a statement (at)	G	L
5	could/would have been	prevented/avoided	G	L
6	considered	all (of) the/my options	G	L
7	had come	down with	G	L
8	to bring up salaries / to bring salaries up	while/whilst	L	G
9	advise you	to send/submit/get	L	G
10	be	a combination of	G	L

Answers — Key word transformation — Test 12

1	having my car / tyre / car tyre	repaired/fixed	G	L
2	increase/grow unless we take	immediate	G	L
3	as not	to miss	G	L
4	makes sense	to	L	G
5	can't/cannot be bothered	to work	G	L
6	(to) break	the ice	G	L
7	would (still) eat meat	if	L	G
8	no matter	how hard I	L	G
9	need to be	worked out	G	L
10	in failure	due/owing	G	L

Answers — Key word transformation — Test 13

1	have called	in sick	G	L
2	was making/made	fun of the way / fun of how	G	L
3	sake of	convenience/ease	G	L
4	spite of	(the) criticism	G	L
5	had been	in stock	G	L
6	(course) application	was/has been declined	L	G
7	not catch	what was being	L	G
8	go into	more/greater depth	G	L
9	absolutely no	regrets about	G	L
10	get	straight to the	G	L

Answers — Key word transformation — Test 14

1	hear	the children laughing	L	G
2	appreciate	you talking / you ignoring me / being ignored	L	G
3	(much) more of a	challenge	G	L
4	boasted	that she had met / about having met	L	G
5	have	turned up	G	L
6	denied	telling him/Richard	L	G
7	put	me off	L	G
8	get round to	(doing) it	L	G
9	adapted/changed/altered	to suit	L	G
10	the sight of	Sara (performing)	L	G

Answers — Key word transformation — Test 15

1	taste	in	L	G
2	was such a	relief to	G	L
3	unsuitable/inappropriate	source of information / information source	L	G
4	said to have	disliked working	G	L
5	keeping	an eye on	G	L
6	what / the thing (that)	matters (the)	G	L
7	few athletes who/that	compete / are competing / keep competing / continue	G	L
8	are more likely	to find/gain	G	L
9	is about to	give/deliver/make/start	G	L
10	not supposed to	tell / have told	G	L

Answers — Key word transformation — Test 16

1	in the	long run	G	L
2	regret not	taking / having taken	L	G
3	accused Oana of	finishing	G	L
4	will have	qualified as / received her qualifications	G	L
5	fond memories	of	L	G
6	to cut	back/down	G	L
7	has not been	taken/made	G	L
8	are entitled	to access/join/do	G	L
9	had never flown	before / prior to	G	L
10	made it	difficult/hard/impossible for	G	L

Answers — Key word transformation — Test 17

1	got/was	(too) carried away	L	G
2	cannot/can't stand	writing / having to write	L	G
3	must be	taken/adopted/found	G	L
4	have the right	to park	L	G
5	tend to	have/get/attract/receive	G	L
6	took / really took	off	L	G
7	told Isla not to	contact/call/phone/ring	G	L
8	is trying	to find/get	G	L
9	was tempted	to book/have/take	L	G
10	no such thing	as	G	L

Answers — Key word transformation — Test 18

1	will be / is going to be / is due to be	published	G	L
2	keeping/bearing	in mind (that)	G	L
3	has come	up with	L	G
4	same (amount/level of) strength	as	L	G
5	higher/better/greater	chance of survival	G	L
6	no intention(s)	of changing/altering	G	L
7	provided us with	everything / what / the information	L	G
8	will die	out	G	L
9	had not	been wearing	G	L
10	has successfully combined	rock and/with	G	L

Answers — Key word transformation — Test 19

#				
1	lack the determination	to be/become	L	G
2	was formerly	known	G	L
3	will be forced	to take/do/get	G	L
4	is always	open to / willing to try	L	G
5	not put	(so much) pressure	G	L
6	was	out of breath	G	L
7	a positive influence	on	L	G
8	are sold	separately from	G	L
9	had never/not thought	about/of	G	L
10	might have / possibly	made it/everything up	G	L

Answers — Key word transformation — Test 20

#				
1	in agreement	on/about/over what / concerning	L	G
2	hesitate	to contact me if	L	G
3	smartest pair that	you can	L	G
4	which	proved to / turned out to / I found to	G	L
5	providing (that)	you give/send us	L	G
6	was	limited to	G	L
7	made up for	missing	L	G
8	the most convenience	when/while/if	L	G
9	took pleasure in	hitting	L	G
10	could/would have	beaten/defeated	G	L

Notes

Notes

Notes

www.ingramcontent.com/pod-product-compliance
Lightning Source LLC
Chambersburg PA
CBHW081918090526
44590CB00019B/3400